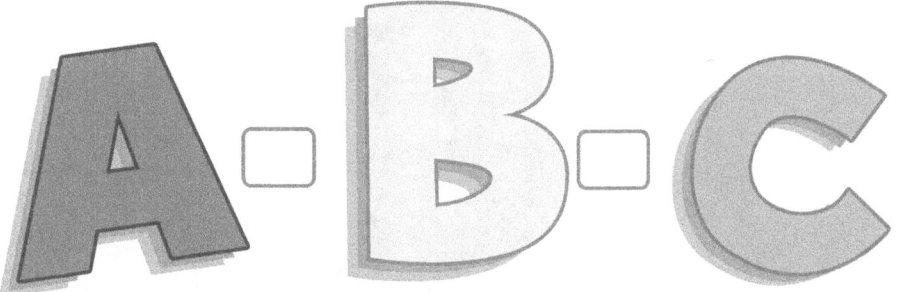

Alphabet Workbook

by Allison Hall

Quail Publishers

Quail Publishers

Published by
Quail Publishers L.L.C
info@quailpublishers.com
www.quailpublishers.com

The publisher grants teachers permission to photocopy pages from this book for classroom use only. No other part of this publication may be reproduced, stored in a retrieval system or transmitted in any form or by any means, electronic, mechanical, photocopying, recording or otherwise, without the prior permission of the publisher.
All verses are adaptations from the Authorized King James Version of The Holy Bible.

Written by Allison Hall
Cover and Interior design by Earl Roumell
Interior illustrations by Pete McDaniel and Earl Roumell
Education Consultant: Gertrude McKenzie
Editor: Keisha Hall

ISBN: 978-0-9894627-0-9

Copyright © 2014 by Allison Hall. All rights reserved
Printed in the U.S.A.

Contents

Introduction 4
Teaching with Bible Phonics: A-B-C 5
Other Alphabet Recognition Activities 6
Suggested Songs 7
The Activity Sheets
Letter A 8-9
Letter B 10-11
Letter C 12-13
Letter D 14-15
Letter E 16-17
Letter F 18-19
Letter G 20-21
Letter H 22-23
Letter I 24-25
Letter J 26-27
Letter K 28-29
Letter L 30-31
Letter M 32-33
Letter N 34-35
Letter O 36-37
Letter P 38-39
Letter Q 40-41
Letter R 42-43
Letter S 44-45
Letter T 46-47
Letter U 48-49
Letter V 50-51
Letter W 52-53
Letter X 54-55
Letter Y 56-57
Letter Z 58-59
Revision Exercises
Write the Alphabet 60
Letter Shapes 61
My Alphabet Poster 62
Word Challenge 63

INTRODUCTION

Alphabet recognition, knowing the letters and the sounds they represent, is a very important step for young children who are just learning to read. Bible Phonics: A-B-C is the ideal workbook to help them to recognize and form all letters of the alphabet, whilst learning more about the Bible. The book also has phonemic awareness activities that help children to learn the letter sounds.

The activity sheets allow children to identify and form all the letters in upper- and lowercase forms. The alliterative sentences help children to learn the sounds of all the letters of the alphabet and experience stories in the Bible. For example, the alliterative sentence, "*The woman walks to the well*" introduces the sound of the letter 'w', as well as the story about Jesus and the Samaritan woman at the well (John 4:8).

These engaging, multisensory activities provide children with the opportunities to build letter recognition, letter sound relationships and letter formation skills. Bible Phonics: A-B-C book fully supports the early childhood and children's Bible study curriculums.

The activities provided in the book will help children to:

- Learn the initial letter sounds.
- Distinguish between upper- and lowercase letters (capital and small letters).
- Distinguish between letters that look alike, for example, 'b' and 'd'.
- Trace letters and write others on their own.
- Develop their vocabulary.
- Learn more about the Bible.

TEACHING WITH BIBLE PHONICS A-B-C

Teaching Letter Sounds

Learning the sounds of spoken language is very important for young children to become excellent readers. Alliteration is a great strategy to teach phonemic awareness. The use of alliteration allows children to learn the sounds of all the letters of the alphabet. This pre-reading skill is needed for children to understand the alphabetic principle – that letters represent sounds and these sounds can be blended to form words.

Teaching Letter Formation

Letter formation is an important component of handwriting instruction. It fosters automatic letter recognition, builds fine motor skills and develops children's confidence. These are critical elements needed for success in reading and writing. For letter formation to be effective, children should not only be provided with the proper writing tool, but also be shown the proper formation of each letter. When children use the activity sheets in this book they learn to form letters properly and gain the experience needed to develop beautiful and legible handwriting.

How to use the Bible Phonics: A-B-C activity sheets

The activity sheets can be used in a variety of ways depending on your curriculum and the needs of the children you teach.

Before the lesson

1. Review the letter you will be teaching.
2. Read the Bible story relating to each alliterative sentence.
3. Make sure that children have the necessary stationery and resources to participate in the lesson.
4. Develop an exciting and engaging lesson which allows for multisensory activities.

During the lesson

5. Read the instructions to children.
6. Use the alliterative sentences to teach letter sounds and as memory gems.
7. Use the activity sheets to teach the letter sounds and letter formation. You should model the proper mouth position that is needed to say each letter sound correctly. Make sure that you also demonstrate the sequence in which each letter is formed.
8. Use a song and a Bible story relating to each main picture as reinforcement strategies. You can also have students make art and craft projects to further support the letter being taught.

OTHER ALPHABET RECOGNITION ACTIVITIES

Alphabet Hunt

Alphabet Hunt is a great way to help children to remember the letter shapes. Ask them to observe their environment and identify things that have similar shapes as letters of the alphabet. You can take them for a walk around the school or community to identify things with similar shapes as the letters.

For example: the fading moon ☾ looks like a 'c' and a hula hoop ◯ looks like an 'o'.

Alphabet Aerobics

Alphabet Aerobics is an exciting way to use play and movement to promote learning. Through play children develop their motor skills and are taught healthy lifestyles. Engage children in an alphabet aerobics class where they use their bodies to make letter shapes. They can also use objects such as the hula-hoop to help them form difficult letters such as 'b' and 'p'.

Children making letters 't', 'x' and 'b'

Suggested Songs

Songs are very powerful teaching tools. They help to create an environment that is conducive to learning, and make lessons more meaningful and exciting. The rhythm, repetition and predictable nature of songs help children build their vocabulary and remember information.
Below is a list of some great songs to strengthen your lesson. You can access the lyrics and rhythm of these songs on the Internet and on our website.

- ♪ A to Z with Noah
- ♪ Esther
- ♪ Five loaves and two fish
- ♪ Give me oil in my lamp
- ♪ Little David play on your harp
- ♪ I will make you fishers of men
- ♪ J-E-S-U-S
- ♪ Jesus loves the little children
- ♪ Jesus wants me for a sunbeam
- ♪ The Alphabet Song
- ♪ The Ants go Marching
- ♪ Zacchaeus was a wee little man

Aa

Name _____

Trace the letters. Then write some on your own.

ant

Be **a**s wise **a**s **a**n **a**nt.
Proverbs 6:6

Bible Phonics: A-B-C Activity Sheets Quail Publishers L.L.C

Name _____

A

a

Write the letter 'a' to complete the words.

__nt   __nt

Say the name of each picture. Then place a circle around those that have the short 'a' sound.

Place a circle around the apples with 'A' and 'a'.

A V A M
o a d a

Color the letters.

Aa

Quail Publishers L.L.C   Bible Phonics: A-B-C Activity Sheets

Bb

Name _____

Trace the letters. Then write some on your own.

B B B B B

basket

b b b b b b b b b

Baby Moses is in the **b**asket **b**y the river **b**ank.
Exodus 2:3

Bible Phonics: A-B-C Activity Sheets   Quail Publishers L.L.C

Name _____

Write the letter 'b' to complete the words.

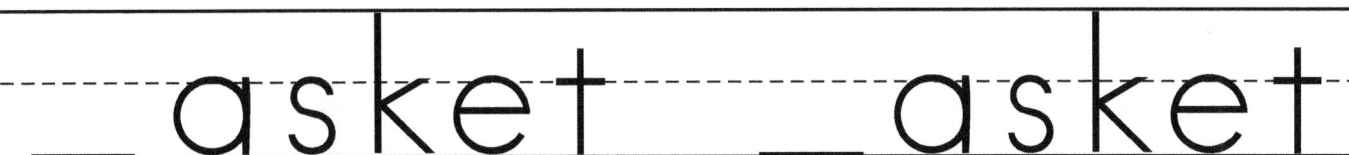

Say the name of each picture. Then place a circle around those that have the /b/ sound.

 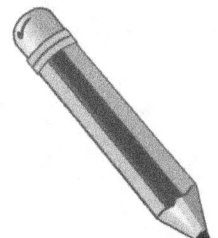 

Place a circle around the books with 'B' and 'b'.	Color the letters.
B B P b g b	B b

Quail Publishers L.L.C   Bible Phonics:A-B-C Activity Sheets

Cc

Name _____

Trace the letters. Then write some on your own.

C C C C C

camel

C c c c c c c c c

A **c**aravan of **c**amels **c**arries Rebekah to **C**anaan.
Genesis 24:61

Name _____

C

c

Write the letter 'c' to complete the words.

_amel   _amel

Say the name of each picture. Then place a circle around those with the hard 'c' sound.

  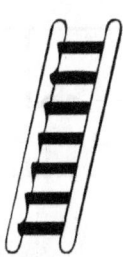

Place a circle around the cats with 'C' and 'c'.

Color the letters.

Cc

Quail Publishers L.L.C

Bible Phonics: A-B-C Activity Sheets 13

Dd

Name _____

Trace the letters. Then write some on your own.

donkey

The **d**onkey falls **d**own on the **d**usty road.
Numbers 22:27

Bible Phonics: A-B-C Activity Sheets
Quail Publishers L.L.C

Name _____

D

d

Write the letter 'd' to complete the words.

__onkey   __onkey

Say the name of each picture. Then place a circle around those that have the /d/ sound.

 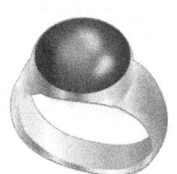 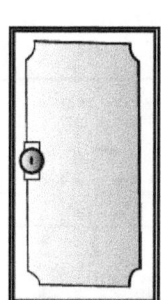

Place a circle around the doors with 'D' and 'd'.	Color the letters.
D B D d p d	Dd

Quail Publishers L.L.C

Bible Phonics: A-B-C Activity Sheets   15

Ee

Name _____

Trace the letters. Then write some on your own.

egg

Owls will enter Edom and lay eggs.
Isaiah 34:15

Bible Phonics: A-B-C Activity Sheets　　　Quail Publishers L.L.C

Name_____

E

e

Write the letter 'e' to complete the words.

_gg   _gg

Say the name of each picture. Then place a circle around those that have the short 'e' sound.

Place a circle around the eggs with 'E' and 'e'.

E F E H
c e o e

Color the letters.

Ee

Quail Publishers L.L.C

Ff

Name _____

Trace the letters. Then write some on your own.

fish

Five loaves and two fish feed five thousand people.
Luke 9:13-16

Bible Phonics: A-B-C Activity Sheets

Quail Publishers L.L.C

Name _____

Write the letter 'f' to complete the words.

__ish   __ish

Say the name of each picture. Then place a circle around those that have the /f/ sound.

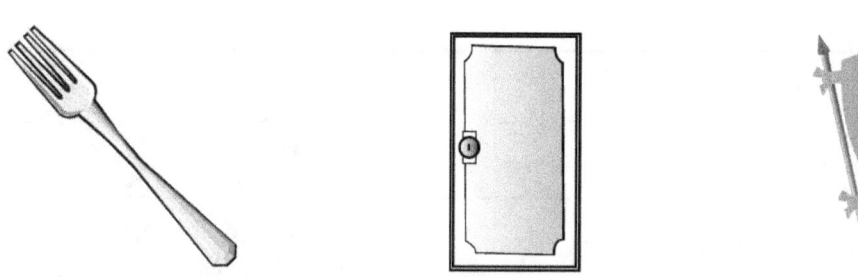

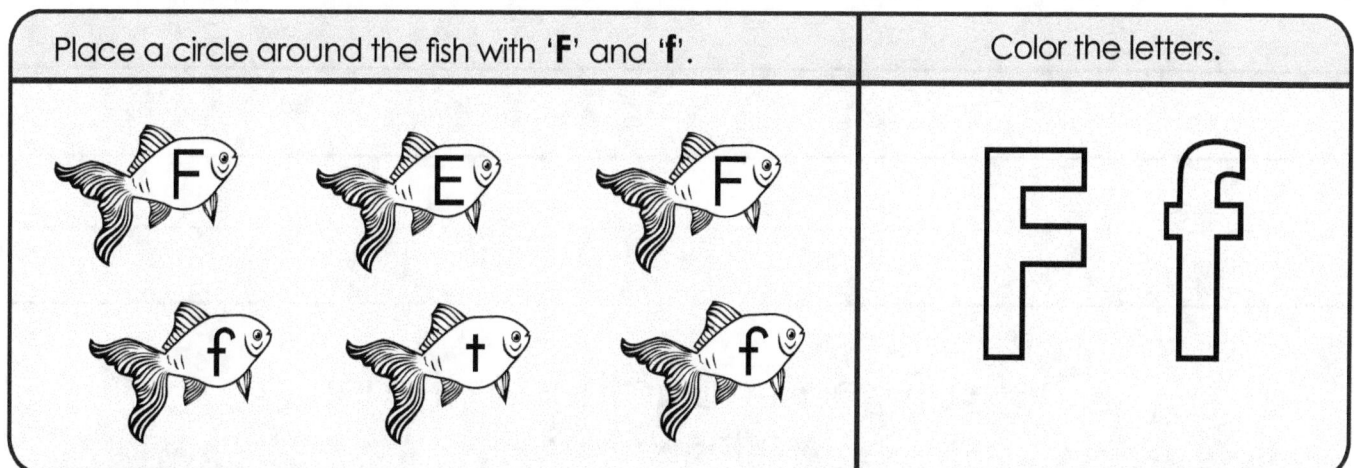

Place a circle around the fish with 'F' and 'f'.   Color the letters.

Quail Publishers L.L.C   Bible Phonics: A-B-C Activity Sheets

Gg

Name _____

Trace the letters. Then write some on your own.

G G G G G

goat

g g g g g g g g g

The **g**ruff **g**oats will **g**ather on the left.
Matthew 25:33

Name _____

G

g

Write the letter 'g' to complete the words.

__oat   __oat

Say the name of each picture. Then place a circle around those that have the hard 'g' sound.

  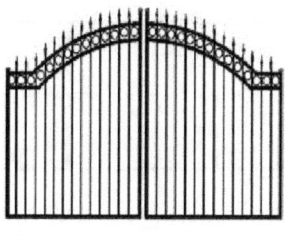

| Place a circle around the goats with 'G' and 'g'. | Color the letters. |

Quail Publishers L.L.C

Bible Phonics: A-B-C Activity Sheets

Hh

Name _____

harp

Trace the letters. Then write some on your own.

David plays his harp to make Saul happy.
1 Samuel 16:23

Bible Phonics: A-B-C Activity Sheets

Quail Publishers L.L.C

Name _____

H

h

Write the letter 'h' to complete the words.

__arp   __arp

Say the name of each picture. Then place a circle around those that have the /h/ sound.

   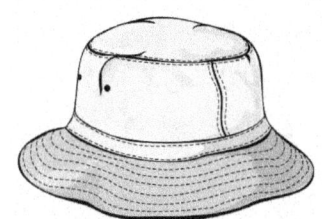   

Place a circle around the hats with 'H' and 'h'.

H   A   H
n   h   h

Color the letters.

Hh

I i

Name _____

Trace the letters. Then write some on your own.

insect

The **i**cky **i**nsects did not hurt the **I**sraelites.
Exodus 8:22

Bible Phonics: A-B-C Activity Sheets   Quail Publishers L.L.C

Name _____

I

i

Write the letter 'i' to complete the words.

__nsect   __nsect

Say the name of each picture. Then place a circle around those that have the short 'i' sound.

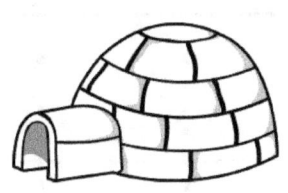  

Place a circle around the igloos with 'I' and 'i'.	Color the letters.
I J I i j i	I i

Jj

Name _____

Trace the letters. Then write some on your own.

J J J J J

Jesus

j j j j j j j j j

Jesus' journey takes him to Jerusalem.
Matthew 21:10

Bible Phonics: A-B-C Activity Sheets   Quail Publishers L.L.C

Name _____

J

j

Write the letter 'J' to complete the words.

__esus __esus

Say the name of each picture. Then place a circle around those that have the /j/ sound.

Place a circle around the jars with 'J' and 'j'.

J I T J
i J j g

Color the letters.

Jj

Quail Publishers L.L.C   Bible Phonics: A-B-C Activity Sheets

Name _____

Kk

Trace the letters. Then write some on your own.

K K K K K

key

K K K K K K K K

King Jesus gives Peter the **k**eys to His **k**ingdom.
St. Matthew 16:19

Bible Phonics: A-B-C Activity Sheets Quail Publishers L.L.C

Name _____

K

k

Write the letter 'k' to complete the words.

__ey   __ey

Say the name of each picture. Then place a circle around those that have the /k/ sound.

Place a circle around the kites with 'K' and 'k'.   Color the letters.

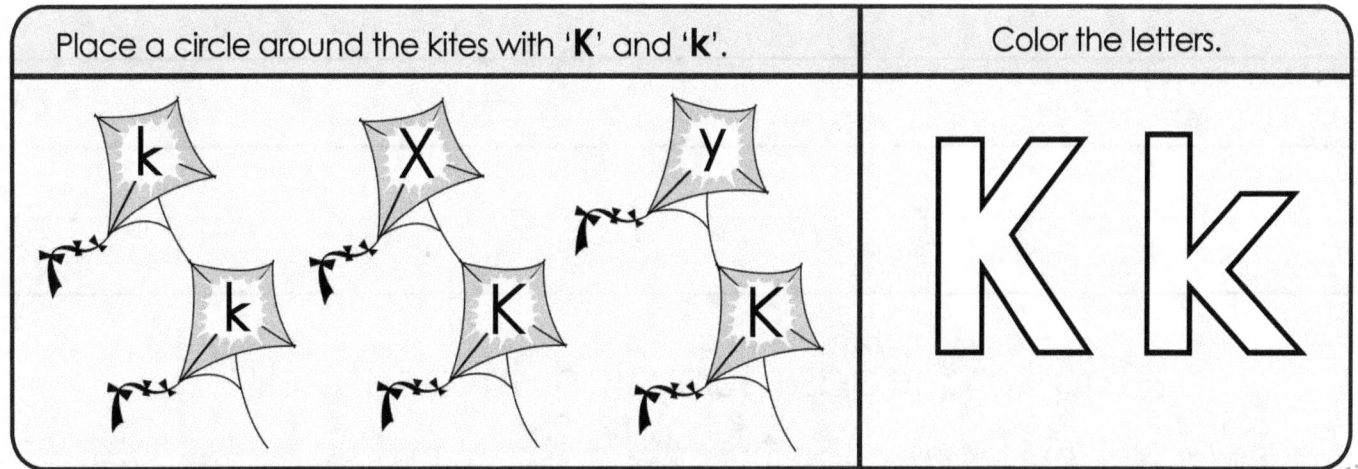

Quail Publishers L.L.C   Bible Phonics: A-B-C Activity Sheets

Name _____

Ll

Trace the letters. Then write some on your own.

lion

The **L**ord **l**eads many **l**ions in the **l**and.
2 Kings 17: 25

Bible Phonics:A-B-C Activity Sheets
Quail Publishers L.L.C

Name _____

Write the letter 'l' to complete the words.

__ion   __ion

Say the name of each picture. Then place a circle around those that have the /l/ sound.

Place a circle around the lambs with 'L' and 'l'.

Color the letters.

Quail Publishers L.L.C

Bible Phonics: A-B-C Activity Sheets

Name _____

Mm

Trace the letters. Then write some on your own.

M M M M M

m m m m m m m

moon

My God **m**ade the **m**oon.
Genesis 1:16

Bible Phonics: A-B-C Activity Sheets   Quail Publishers L.L.C

Name _____

M m

Write the letter '**m**' to complete the words.

___oon   ___oon

Say the name of each picture. Then place a circle around those that have the /**m**/ sound.

 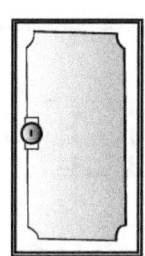 

Place a circle around the mats with '**M**' and '**m**'.	Color the letters.
w m m M N M	M m

Quail Publishers L.L.C   Bible Phonics: A-B-C Activity Sheets 33

Nn

Name _____

Trace the letters. Then write some on your own.

nail

Thomas **n**eeds to see the **n**ail prints.
John 20:24-25

Bible Phonics: A-B-C Activity Sheets Quail Publishers L.L.C

Name _____

N

n

Write the letter 'n' to complete the words.

_ail   _ail

Say the name of each picture. Then place a circle around those that have the /n/ sound.

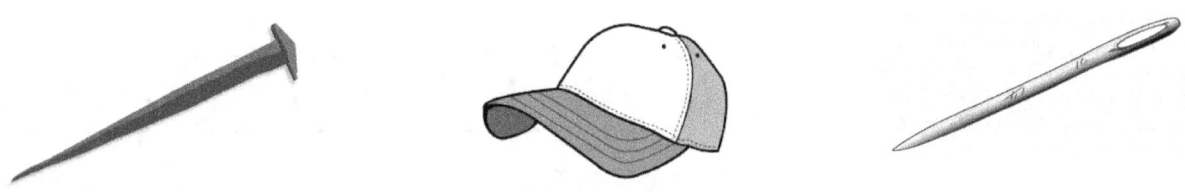

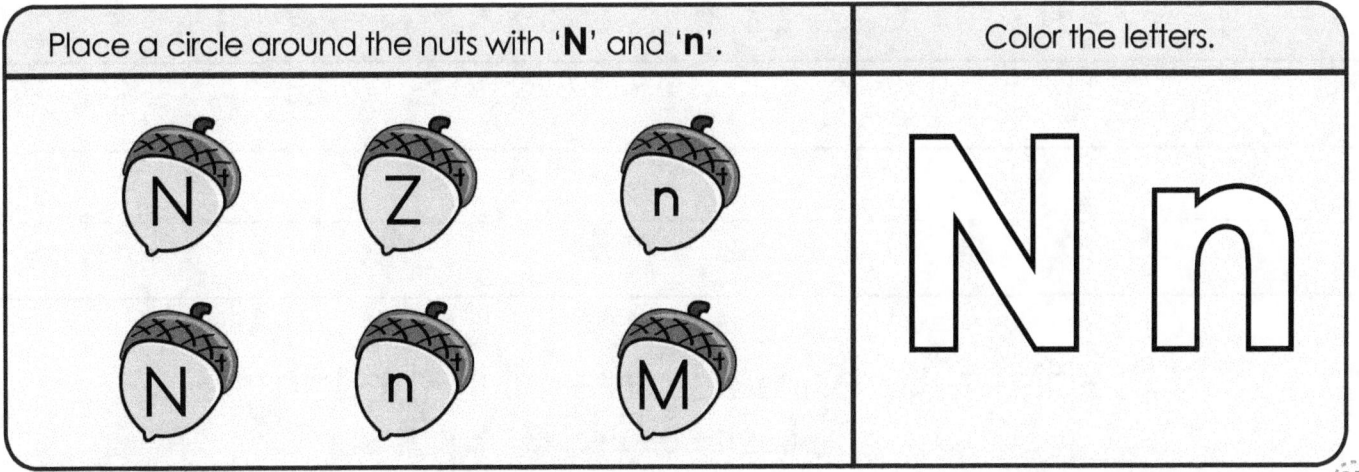

Quail Publishers L.L.C

Bible Phonics: A-B-C Activity Sheets 35

Name _____

Trace the letters. Then write some on your own.

olive

Obedient Aaron puts **o**live oil in the lamps.
Leviticus 24:1-3

Name _____

O o

o

Write the letter 'o' to complete the words.

__live   __live

Say the name of each picture. Then place a circle around those that have the short 'o' sound.

   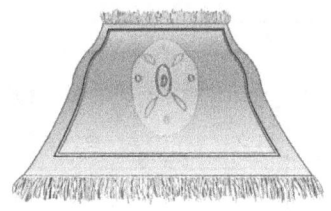   

Place a circle around the onions with 'O' and 'o'.

O Q O
o b o

Color the letters.

O O

Quail Publishers L.L.C   Bible Phonics:A-B-C Activity Sheets 37

Pp

Name _____

Trace the letters. Then write some on your own.

pig

The **p**igs **p**lunge over a high **p**lace.
Matthew 8:32

Bible Phonics: A-B-C Activity Sheets   Quail Publishers L.L.C

Name _____

P

p

Write the letter '**p**' to complete the words.

__ig　　　　　__ig

Say the name of each picture. Then place a circle around those that have the /**p**/ sound.

Place a circle around the pumpkins with '**P**' and '**p**'.　　　Color the letters.

P　B　P
P　b　P

P p

Quail Publishers L.L.C　　　　　Bible Phonics: A-B-C Activity Sheets

Name _____

Qq

Trace the letters. Then write some on your own.

queen

Queen Esther is **qu**ite **qu**ick to help.
Esther 7:3-4

Bible Phonics: A-B-C Activity Sheets

Quail Publishers L.L.C

Name _____

Q

q

Write the letter 'q' to complete the words.

__ueen   __ueen

Say the name of each picture. Then place a circle around those that have the /kw/ sounds.

Place a circle around the quails with 'Q' and 'q'.	Color the letters.
Q q p o q Q	Qq

Quail Publishers L.L.C

Bible Phonics: A-B-C Activity Sheets   41

R r

Name _____

Trace the letters. Then write some on your own.

R R R R R

ring

r r r r r r r r

Joseph receives a royal ring from Pharoah.
Genesis 41:42

Bible Phonics: A-B-C Activity Sheets   Quail Publishers L.L.C

Name _____

R

r

Write the letter 'r' to complete the words.

___ing   ___ing

Say the name of each picture. Then place a circle around those that have the /r/ sound.

  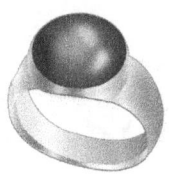

Place a circle around the rabbits with 'R' and 'r'.

B R r
r P R

Color the letters.

Rr

Quail Publishers L.L.C

Bible Phonics: A-B-C Activity Sheets

Ss

Name _____

Trace the letters. Then write some on your own.

S S S S S

sun

S S S S S S S S S

The **s**un **s**tands **s**till in the **s**ky.
Joshua 10:13

Name _____

S

s

Write the letter 's' to complete the words.

_un   _un

Say the name of each picture. Then place a circle around those that have the /s/ sound.

Place a circle around the suns with 'S' and 's'.	Color the letters.
S z S S s z	S s

Quail Publishers L.L.C

Bible Phonics: A-B-C Activity Sheets 45

T t

Name _____

Trace the letters. Then write some on your own.

table

Jesus tosses the tables in the temple.
Matthew 21:12

Bible Phonics: A-B-C Activity Sheets   Quail Publishers L.L.C

Name _____

Write the letter 't' to complete the words.

_able   _able

Say the name of each picture. Then place a circle around those that have the /t/ sound.

 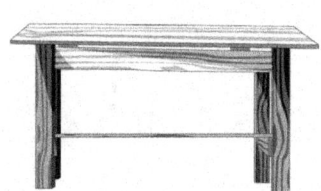 

Place a circle around the tomatoes with 'T' and 't'.

Color the letters.

Uu

Name _____

Trace the letters. Then write some on your own.

Uzzah

God is **u**pset with **U**zzah.
2 Samuel 6:7

Bible Phonics: A-B-C Activity Sheets Quail Publishers L.L.C

Name _____

U

u

Write the letter 'U' to complete the words.

__zzah   __zzah

Say the name of each picture. Then place a circle around those that have the short 'u' sound.

Place a circle around the umbrellas with 'U' and 'u'.	Color the letters.
v u U u U v	U u

Quail Publishers L.L.C   Bible Phonics: A-B-C Activity Sheets 49

Vv

Name _____

vines

Trace the letters. Then write some on your own.

The vineyard is very full of vines.
Isaiah 5:2

Bible Phonics: A-B-C Activity Sheets   Quail Publishers L.L.C

Name _____

V _____

V _____

Write the letter 'v' to complete the words.

__ines   __ines

Say the name of each picture. Then place a circle around those that have the /v/ sound.

Place a circle around the vans with 'V' and 'v'.	Color the letters.
V A v W v V	V v

Quail Publishers L.L.C   Bible Phonics: A-B-C Activity Sheets

Name _____

W w

Trace the letters. Then write some on your own.

W W W W W W

well

w w w w w w w w

The **w**oman **w**alks to the **w**ell.
John 4:6-7

Name _____

-1 2 3 4
W

1 2 3 4
w

Write the letter 'w' to complete the words.

__ell   __ell

Say the name of each picture. Then place a circle around those that have the /w/ sound.

Place a circle around 'W' and 'w' in the worm. | Color the letters.

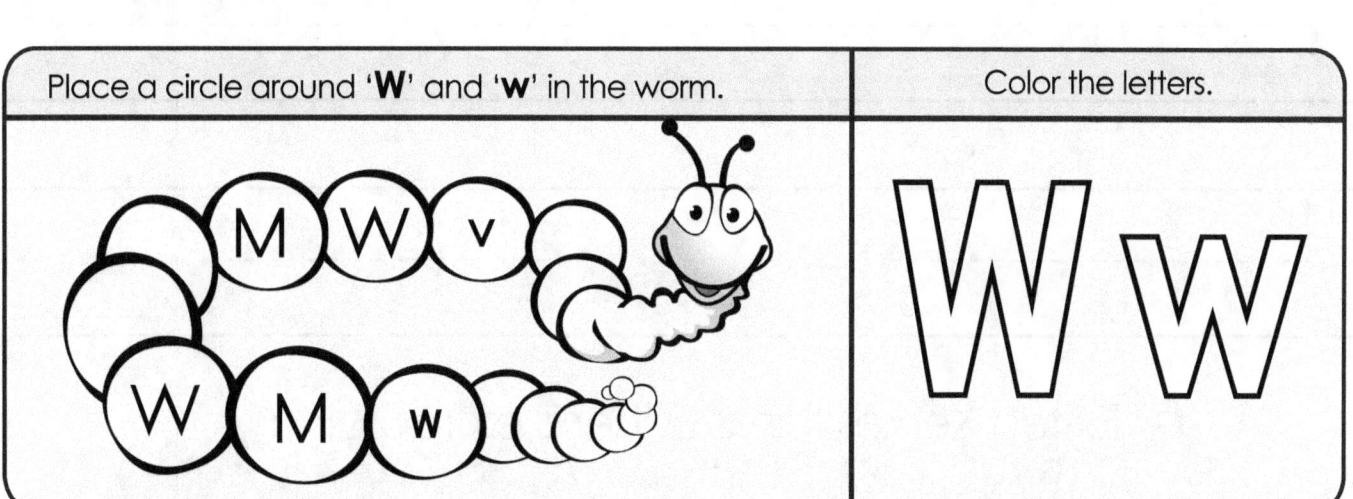

Quail Publishers L.L.C   Bible Phonics:A-B-C Activity Sheets 53

Name _____

Xx

Trace the letters. Then write some on your own.

X X X X X

Xerxes

X x x x x x x x

Exited Xerxes thinks Esther is extraordinary.
Esther 2:17

Bible Phonics:A-B-C Activity Sheets　　　Quail Publishers L.L.C

Name _____

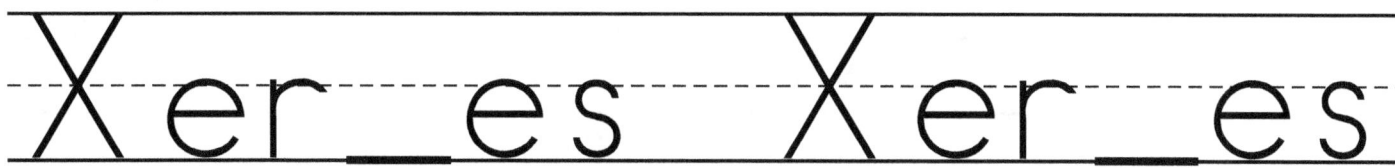

Write the letter '**X**' to complete the words.

Xer_es   Xer_es

Say the name of each picture. Then place a circle around those that have the /**ks**/ sounds.

 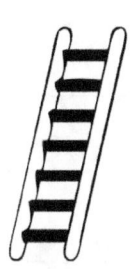 

Place a circle around the boxes with '**X**' and '**x**'.	Color the letters.
[X] [Y] [x] [x] [x] [Y]	X x

Quail Publishers L.L.C   Bible Phonics: A-B-C Activity Sheets

Name _____

Y y

Trace the letters. Then write some on your own.

Y Y Y Y Y

yoke

y y y y y y y y

Hananiah yanks the yoke.
Jeremiah 28:10

Name _____

Y

y

Write the letter 'y' to complete the words.

__oke   __oke

Say the name of each picture. Then place a circle around those that have the /y/ sound.

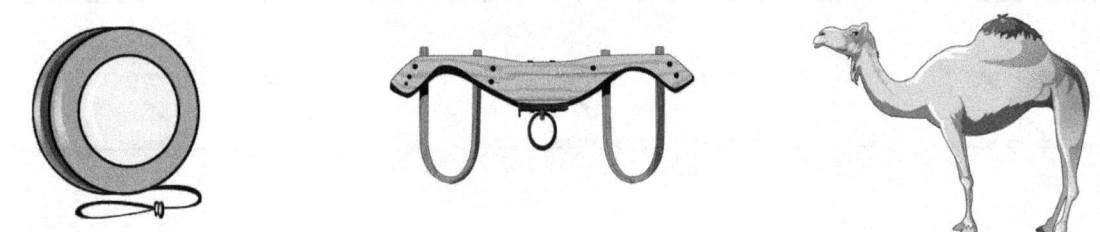

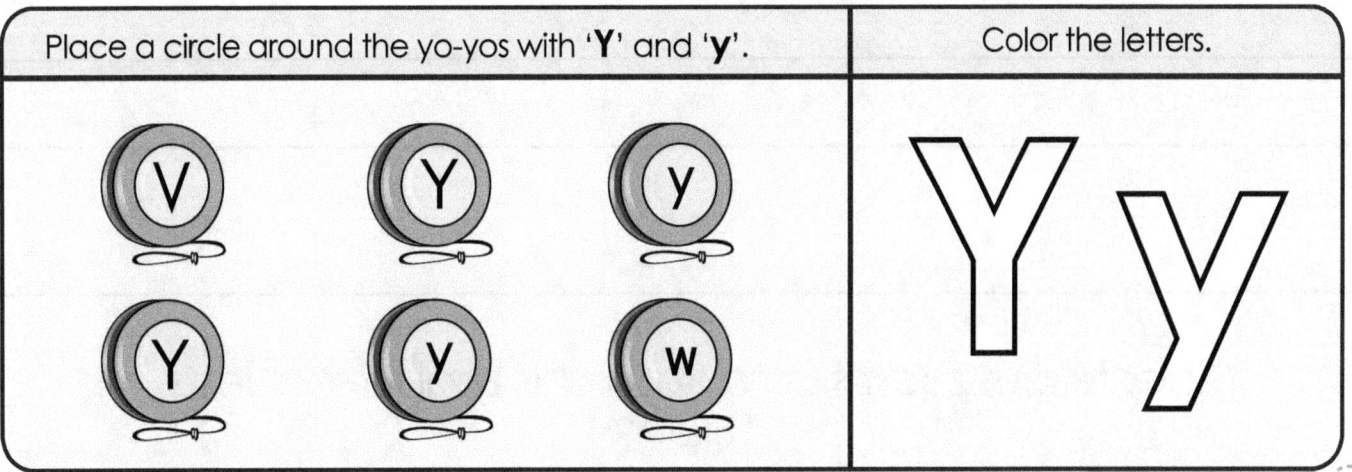

Place a circle around the yo-yos with 'Y' and 'y'.

Color the letters.

Quail Publishers L.L.C   Bible Phonics: A-B-C Activity Sheets 57

Name _____

Zz

Trace the letters. Then write some on your own.

Z Z Z Z Z Z

Zacchaeus

Z z z z z z z z z z

Zacchaeus **z**ooms up a tree in his **z**eal to see Jesus.
Luke 19:1-4

Name _____

Z

Z

Write the letter 'Z' to complete the word.

___acchaeus

Say the name of each picture. Then place a circle around those that have the /z/ sound.

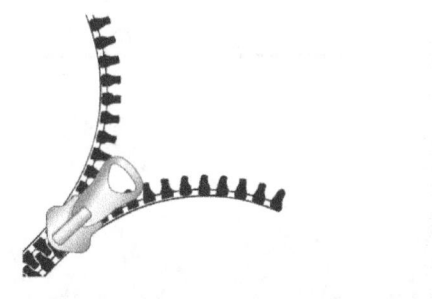  

Place a circle around the zebras with 'Z' and 'z'.	Color the letters.
Z N Z z n z	Z z

Quail Publishers L.L.C

Bible Phonics: A-B-C Activity Sheets

Name _____

WRITE THE ALPHABET

THE ALPHABET Write the missing letters of the alphabet in **upper-** and **lowercase** forms.

Aa

Zz

Name _____

LETTER SHAPES

The objects below have shapes that are similar to letters in the alphabet. **Write the correct letter beside the object it resembles.** One has been done for you.

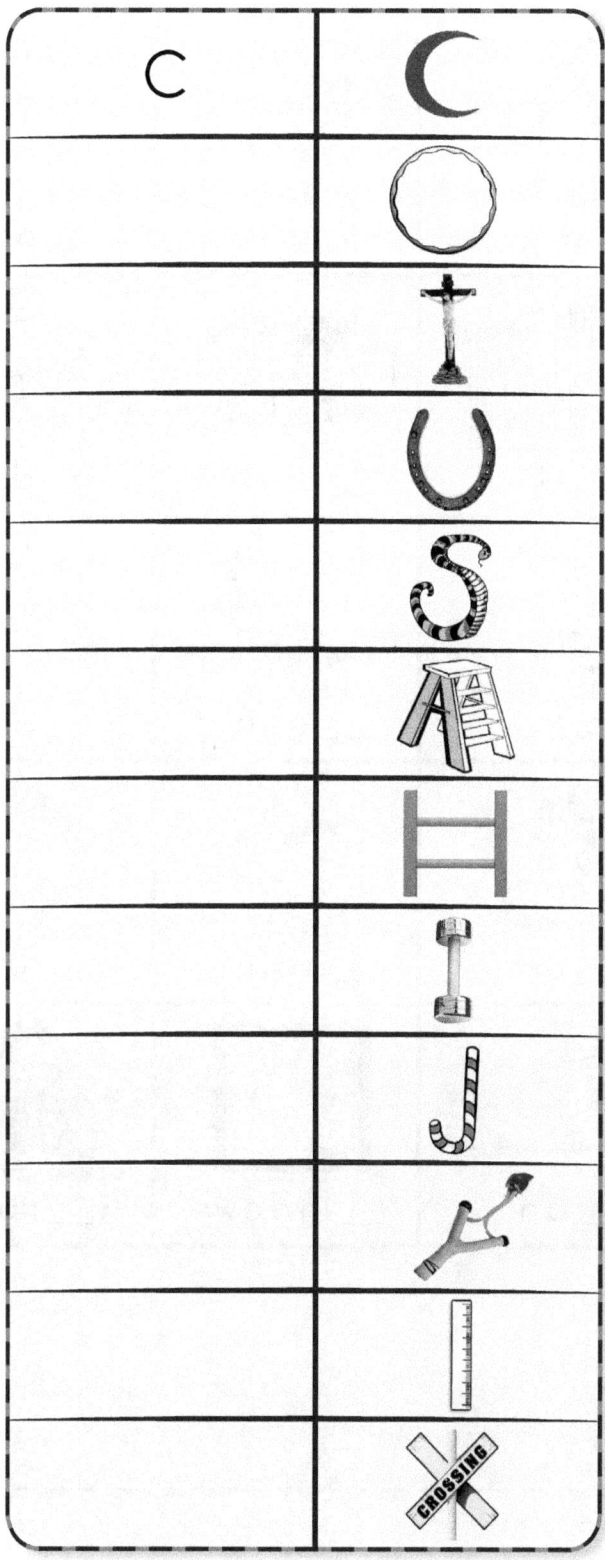

Quail Publishers L.L.C   Bible Phonics: A-B-C Activity Sheets

Name_____

MY ALPHABET POSTER

Say the name of each picture. Then write the correct letter to complete each word.

__pple	__ag	__ow	__oor	__gg
__an	__ate	__ouse	__gloo	__ug
__ey	__adder	__oon	__eedle	__range
__ig	__ueen	__abbit	__un	__able
__mbrella	__an	__indow	__ray	__o-yo
__ebra				

Bible Phonics: A-B-C Activity Sheets

Quail Publishers L.L.C

WORD CHALLENGE

Try to remember the sounds of the letters of the alphabet. Say them all again, then say the words below.

-ad	-am	-an	-ap	-at	-en	-et
bad	dam	Dan	cap	cat	Ben	let
dad	ham	fan	lap	fat	hen	jet
had	ram	man	map	mat	men	pet
lad	Sam	pan	rap	pat	pen	vet
sad	tam	ran	tap	rat	ten	wet

-ig	-ip	-og	-ot	-ug	-ut
big	dip	fog	dot	bug	but
fig	hip	hog	got	hug	cut
rig	lip	jog	hot	jug	gut
pig	rip	log	lot	mug	hut
wig	tip		pot	rug	nut

www.ingramcontent.com/pod-product-compliance
Lightning Source LLC
Chambersburg PA
CBHW060519300426

44112CB00017B/2732